Conemaugh Valley Elementary Library

what you will learn from this book

A good jump shooter must be a good leaper? Not true. The height of the jump is not very important. There are some things about the jump that are important. These are related in the pages ahead.

Coaches want their players to shoot lay-ups off a certain foot because they want them to be able to use either hand? Nope. Coaches want this but the reason for it is not what is commonly thought.

The lay-up should be a must shot. You will learn how to do this by reading this book.

the jump shot and lay-up

text/Paul J. Deegan
illustrations/
Harold Henriksen

Consultant: Lloyd Raymond, B.A., Augsburg College; M.S., Physical Education, Mankato State College; Instructor in Physical Education and Head Basketball Coach, Mankato State College.

CREATIVE EDUCATION
Mankato, Minnesota

Published by Creative Educational Society, Inc., 123 South Broad Street, Mankato, Minnesota 56001. Copyright © 1975 by Creative Educational Society, Inc. International copyrights reserved in all countries. No part of this book may be reproduced in any form without written permission from the publisher. Printed in the United States. Distributed by Childrens Press, 1224 West Van Buren Street, Chicago, Illinois 60607.
Library of Congress Number: 75-11680   ISBN O-87191-432-8
Library of Congress Cataloging in Publication Data
Deegan, Paul J.   1937-
   The jump shot.
   SUMMARY: Describes the technique and importance of the jumpshot in basketball.
   1. Basketball—Juvenile literature. (1. Basketball) I. Henriksen, Harold. II. Title.
GV885.1.D42   796.32'32   75-11680   ISBN: O-87191-432-8

For Lisa, Mike, and John – may participation in athletics bring you as much enjoyment as it has brought your dad.

jump shot for older player

They all shoot the jumper — Walt Frazier, Julius Irving, Bob McAdoo. Jerry West did. Oscar Robertson did. If you go to a professional or college or high school game, it's likely to be the only shot you'll see taken from the floor.

The jump shot is favored by basketball players because it's the shot you can get off quickest. You also need less room to shoot it than the set shot. A defender can come up and distract or block a set shot after you have begun your shooting motion. The defender doesn't have enough time to do this if the jumper is shot properly.

Few players will have the proper size and strength or coordination to be able to shoot a jump shot properly before the last part of their seventh grade year. Lacking size and strength, the younger player finds it very difficult to shoot in a relaxed manner or to develop a fluid motion.

If you wonder whether you're an exception, the answer is probably not. If you are not able to do something properly, the only thing you're going to do if you try it anyway is pick up many bad habits. Later, you will have to break these habits if you can.

When it is time for you to begin shooting a jump shot, hopefully you will have already been working on the one-handed set shot or push shot, the basic shot in basketball. The fundamentals involved in shooting a jump shot are also those that are used in the set shot.

The body must be under control before the shot. The knees are bent to provide power for the shot and, now, the jump as well. The body leans slightly forward.

The ball is held with the fingertips of the shooting hand on the lower back of the ball. The hand position is somewhat to the right on the ball if you're right-handed. The thumb and the index finger (the finger next to the thumb) form a V. The other hand is held on the side of the ball, toward the bottom, until you shoot. This hand balances the ball and helps protect the ball from defensive players.

The ball is held in front of you between the shoulder and the eye on your shooting side. The elbow on that side is in close to the body and slightly in front of your wrist. The elbow must be in a direct line with the basket.

The differences in shooting the jump shot will be that the feet are likely to be in a straight line before the shot, not one foot slightly ahead of the other. The front foot (the left foot for a righthander) is not likely to be at much of an angle to the back one. Both feet are likely to be more under the body or spread less than shoulder width.

The important thing is not exactly where the feet are placed, but whether or not you are in a comfortable position with good body balance.

The most important difference in the jump shot, of course, is that the shooter jumps before shooting the ball. The jump shooter must learn to jump straight up. The jump must also be in line with the basket. The jump must enable the shooter to face the basket; it cannot turn him away from it. Going straight up provides good body control and ensures that the ball can be shot from the same position each time.

It is not important how high you jump. This would be important only if you were trying to shoot over a much taller man. Even in this case, the advantage of the jump shot is not the height from which you shoot. The shot is intended to free you from the defender. The quickness and the surprise of the shot accomplish this. The jump shot is deceptive. You can stop and shoot off the dribble or go up quickly while stationary. In neither case does your defender know when you're going to go up.

Sometimes jump shooters will jump to the side to free themselves from defenders. However, going straight up should always be your goal.

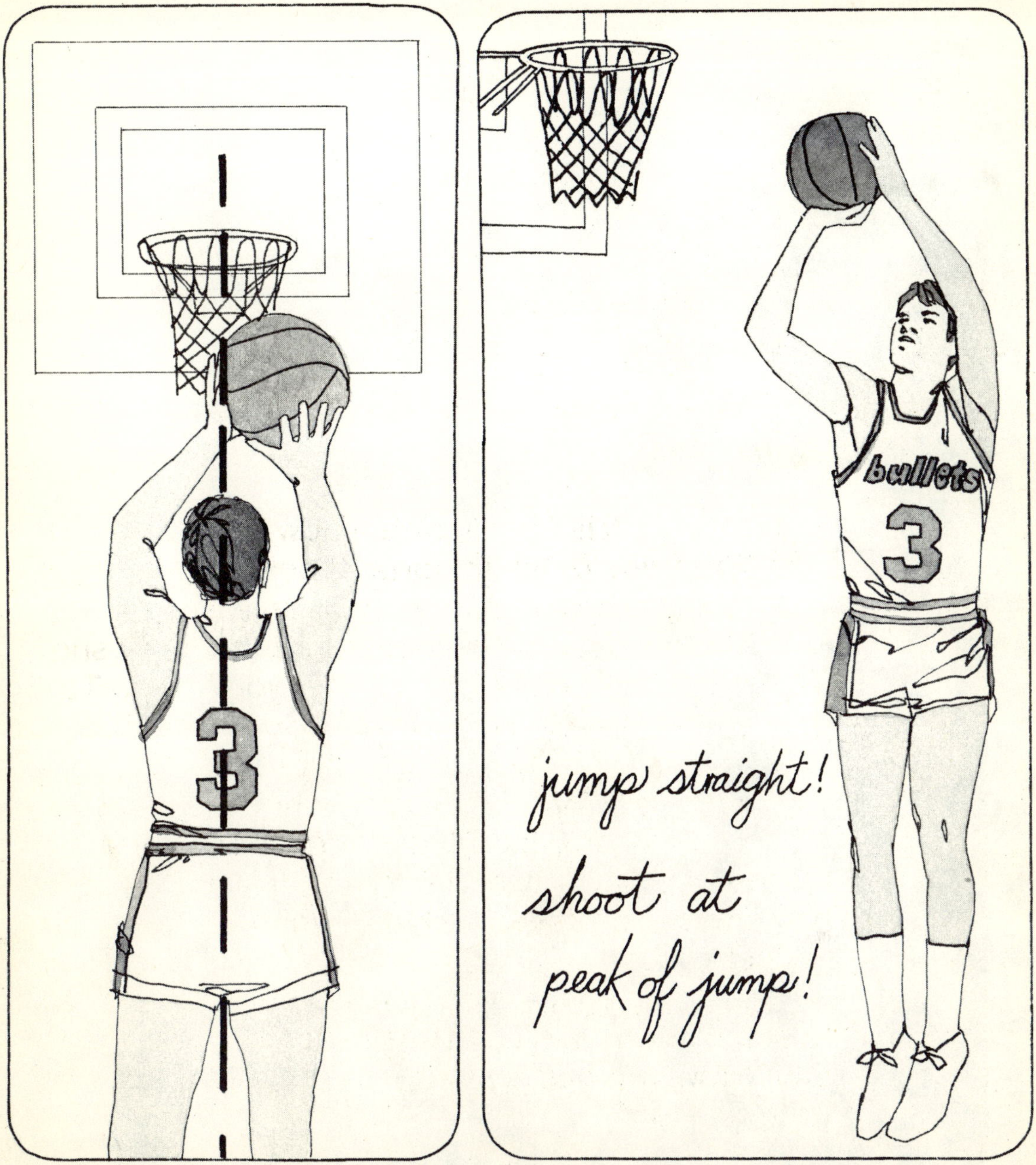

*jump straight!
shoot at
peak of jump!*

Jerry West was as good a jump shooter as anyone who has played the game. A couple of years ago, the Los Angeles Laker star had trouble shooting during the final round of the National Basketball Association play-offs. Later, he realized that his shooting was off because he was not going straight up on his jump.

West used to practice by putting a piece of tape on the floor and jumping from that spot, concentrating on coming down exactly on the same spot. It's difficult to fall backward when you go up because your body momentum is pushing you forward. However, most jump shooters will land slightly ahead of the place where they took off. Going straight up as West tried to do gives you the most height, saves important fractions of a second in shooting, and provides better body and ball control.

It is very important to release the ball at the top of your jump. At this point you are actually suspended in the air for a moment. For a moment, you have good balance. If you shoot on the way down, you throw off your balance and your aim.

The release of the ball on a jump shot is the same as for the set shot except that the ball is released higher. For most players, the release comes right at the top of the head. The exact point — forehead level or four inches higher — will vary from player to player. Avoid bringing the ball back over the head. The ball must be shot from out in front of the body.

PEAK OF JUMP

correct

incorrect

wrist and elbow position important

Just before release, cock your wrist, which is behind your elbow. The wrist must be relaxed. It is loose but not limp. When you release the ball, snap your wrist, which by now has moved ahead of the elbow, to provide follow through. The ball is flipped off your fingertips, creating backspin for control. Your index finger comes off the ball last and is pointed toward the basket, helping give direction to the shot.

Watch a good jump shooter — one who makes about 50 percent of his shots. You will notice that this player's arm motion and the place where the ball is held are the same on every shot. The player may jump higher one time. He or she may even get forced to one side or another on the jump. But each time the player will shoot the ball exactly the same way. This should be your goal, too.

Don't forget to arc the ball on your shot. The ball must come down into the 10-foot high basket. Most jump shooters use less arc than when they shoot a set shot. A very flat shot will fire off the rim or backboard and will seldom bounce around and in.

Concentration is extremely important. You must have your eyes locked on the basket from the moment you begin your jump. Keep them on the basket until the shot is made or bounces away. You must also learn to shoot to a specific spot on the basket.

Your choices are the middle of the basket or the hole as it's called, the spot just over the front of the rim, or the back of the rim. Most coaches and shooters prefer either the hole or the spot just over the front of the rim. You'll have to decide what works best for you.

lay-up

A very important shot, one which most players treat too casually, is the lay-up. Almost every team warms up for a game by shooting lay-ups. Still, many are missed.

It is such an important shot because it is usually an easy shot. When you're that close to the basket, you shouldn't miss. One pro coach says 99 percent of lay-ups should be made.

The lay-up, too, presents a problem for the small youngster. We'll consider this problem later. The lay-up involves two things — leaving the floor and going to the basket is one; the shot is the other.

The takeoff and the jump on the lay-up are very important. Many young players use a long jump approach on a lay-up. They take off too soon. The object is not to see how long you can stay in the air. It is how close you can get your hand to the basket.

Therefore, you want a high jump approach. You want to get up as high as you can. The higher you get, the closer you will be to the basket and the less room there will be for error in releasing the ball.

If you want to go up high, you can't start your jump too soon. The exact takeoff spot will vary from player to player depending on each one's size and strength. But it will be three to four feet before you get to the basket.

A check on whether you jumped up rather than forward is the place where you finish after the lay-up. If you're more than two or three feet beyond the basket, you made too much of a long jump rather than a high jump.

Every coach tells his players to take off for a lay-up on their left foot when they're coming from the right side of the basket. You're told to take off on your right foot when coming from the left side. The reason for this is not that you shoot with the right hand on the right side or the left hand on the left side.

The reason is to protect the ball from a defender. If you go off your left foot on the right side, the left side of your body will protect the ball. Coming from the left, your right side will protect the ball if you take off on your right foot.

There's nothing wrong with learning to use your off hand so that you can comfortably use either hand near the basket. You'll be more effective if you can. It is a mark of pride for basketball players to be able to use either hand for a lay-up. But it's not the essential thing in shooting a lay-up. The only important rule that applies to shooting a lay-up is: MAKE IT!

The lay-up shot should be banked off the backboard. As you leap to the basket, carry the ball with both hands, protecting it with your non-shooting hand. Extend your body and arms fully. At the top of your jump, you should be as close to the basket as you can get.

You should approach the basket from an angle if possible because this makes it easier to use the backboard. At the top of your jump, the ball is held the same way it would be if you were going to shoot a jump shot or a set shot. The shooting hand is on the lower back of the ball to the right side (if you're shooting right-handed). The other hand is on the side of the ball. This is the normal shooting position.

The only difference in shooting the lay-up is your arm position. You should reach your arms up as high as you can.

At the top of your jump with your arms way up, release the ball. Lay it on the backboard off your fingertips. Don't flip it off your fingers. LAY it up! Try to lay the ball off the near upper corner of the white rectangle marked behind and above the rim.

Older and taller players sometimes release the ball underhanded on the lay-up. They shoot the ball off the palm of their hand. However, releasing the ball from the normal shooting position gives you more control and therefore greater accuracy.

If you are forced to come directly at the basket from the front, lay the ball off the top middle of the rectangle.

Concentration is also important on a lay-up. Often you're shooting a lay-up off a drive. You've worked hard to get to the basket and you don't force yourself to concentrate on the shot. You blow the basket and a good effort is wasted.

Always work at shooting a lay-up correctly whenever you do it. Never just throw the ball up. Remember, it's a shot you should almost always make.

The problem some young players will have with the lay-up is that they can't really lay the ball up on the board. They are not tall enough for their jump to bring them anywhere near the standard 10-foot-high basket.

The best solution to this problem is to shoot with a junior-sized basketball at a shorter basket. The junior basketball is slightly smaller and gives you better control. An eight-or-nine-foot-high basket enables a young player to shoot with the proper technique. Many school gyms have shorter baskets. Outdoor baskets can be placed on adjustable poles.

If size is a problem and you have to shoot at a standard basket, you will have to "shoot" your lay-up.

The ball is carried through the jump toward the basket in the normal shooting

Conemaugh Valley Elementary Library

position, just as it should be for the normal lay-up. At the top of your jump, instead of laying the ball off your fingertips, shoot it softly. Your target will still be the near upper corner of the rectangle behind the hoop.

A slight flick of the wrist should provide enough power for this lay-up shot. You don't want the ball banging up against the board. You want it to hit softly and bounce down into the basket.

Knowing how to shoot helps but it won't do much good if you don't do it. The boy or girl who wants to be a good basketball player will spend hours practicing shooting. The young player will benefit greatly from using a junior-sized ball and a shorter basket if possible.

Once you know how to shoot the jump shot and the lay-up, the only person who can help you is yourself.

BASEBALL
pitching
hitting
bunting and baserunning

FOOTBALL
passing the football
catching the football
placekicking and punting

BASKETBALL
the set shot
the jump shot
shooting in a game

TENNIS
the basic strokes
serving and returning service
volleying and lobs

HOCKEY
skates and sticks
stickhandling and passing
shooting
checking and defensive play

creative
education
sports
instructional
series for
young
peop*